TABLE OF CONTENTS

Abstract

The growing need to counter improvised explosive devices prompted the resurgence of explosive detection military working dogs in the theater of war and furthered the need for an off-leash requirement in order to increase standoff distance from an unexploded device to allied patrols in the area. History has provided a plethora of evidence to support continued research in the military working dog community to enable Combatant Commander's the ability to have a mission-ready canine force available to counter emerging threats before casualties are incurred. This paper explains why it is necessary, although controversial, to train all DoD explosive detection dogs to the same off-leash standard in order to best provide Combatant Commander's the ability to protect the joint force. It further explains how differing home-station mission sets and improper program alignment promote interservice rivalry and preclude a joint solution. Finally, it offers a series of recommendations to ensure the canine community provides combatant commanders the most capable military working dogs in the world.

"Cry 'Havoc!' and let slip the dogs of war..."[1]
- William Shakespeare

INTRODUCTION

The need to further examine additional capabilities of Military Working Dogs (MWD) in "yet untried ways" was proposed by the Air Force Office of Scientific Research in 1970.[2] Since 2001, the center of this challenge remains the single largest threat to coalition forces engaged in Operation Enduring Freedom--the improvised explosive device (IED).[3] After the invasion of Iraq in 2003, defeating IEDs leveraged against US forces in OEF and OIF became a Combatant Commander (CCDR) priority. The immediate need to counter this growing threat is evidenced in a 2004 Deputy Secretary of Defense action memo establishing a Joint Integrated Process Team (IPT) for Defeating IEDs. In September of that same year, the IPT solution-set included an added off-leash capability for a historically proven weapon of war—the MWD subset, explosive detection dog (EDD).

Sadly, failure to foresee the value of MWDs and their contribution to a count-IED (C-IED) mission years before the tragic events of 9/11, continues a disturbing trend of lessons not learned through the use of canines in war. Today's placement of the DoD MWD program within the Office of the Undersecretary of Defense for Intelligence (OUSD(I)) construct removes it from the eyes of the operators, effectively burying it in a community that cannot and does not most effectively articulate its operational protection value to Combatant Commanders.

---

[1] William Shakespeare. "Julius Caesar," The Literature Network. Last modified 2012, http://www.online-literature.com/shakespeare/julius_caesar/9/.

[2] Air Force Office of Scientific Research, *Conference on Research to Expand the Usefulness of the Military Working Dog,* 1970 (Defense Documentation Center, 1971), i.

[3] U.S. House of Representatives, *The JIEDDO: DoD's Fight Against IEDs Today and Tomorrow,* 2008 (Committee Print, 2008), 9.

This paper will address the MWD community's long-standing fight to obtain and maintain relevance to warfighters and argue the need to promote MWDs as a C-IED enduring capability by realigning the program within the DoD, establishing base-line standards for all explosive detection MWDs and ensuring a steady funding stream in order to provide Combatant Commanders with the most capable tool available anytime, anywhere to safeguard friendly forces against the growing global threat of IEDs.

BACKGROUND

It is an irony that the use of dogs in war can be traced back to the arid land of ancient Mesopotamia, a conflicted region of the world where today's war dogs have returned to ensure the security of the descendants of those who first bred them for battle.[4] From their service at the famed Battle of Marathon to the trenches of WWI, war dogs have served beside foreign armies. It was not until their utility in war was at last realized by the United States during the opening salvos of WWII that the US Army formally established the K9 Corps in May 1942.[5] According to the Patrol Dog Training Branch report in 1970, "an estimated 250,000 dogs were used by all powers for mine detection, casualty, messenger, scout and sentry duty" during WWI alone.[6]

After WWII, the lack of an identifiable need for canines in the armed forces prompted the DoD to end nearly all of its war dog programs.[7] Effects of this decision led to an inability to provide robust support at the outset of the Korean War and began a cycle of drawdown followed by emerging requirements that continues today.[8] The US Army ended its war dog

---

[4] Richard Vargus, "MWDs: A Cost Effective, Low-Tech Answer to a Persistent and Deadly Threat," *Infantry*, April 2011, http://www.highbeam.com/doc/1G1-278773930 html.
[5] Air Force Office of Scientific Research, 13.
[6] Air Force Office of Scientific Research, 13.
[7] Michael Hammerstrom, "Ground Dog Day: Lessons Don't Have to be Relearned in the Use of Dogs in Combat," DTIC Online, Last Modified February 2013. http://www.dtic mil/dtic/tr/fulltext/u2/a442891.pdf.
[8] Hammerstrom, 27.

program after the Korean War, but where the Army dismissed canines for further expeditionary engagement, the Air Force embraced them to secure its bases during the cold war. To this end, the Patrol/Sentry Dog Training Branch, Department of Security Police Training, Lackland AFB, Texas, was established in 1958.[9]

Vietnam brought low intensity conflict to the forefront of the US military lexicon and 4,900 dogs were deployed to engage the unconventional, insurgent threat.[10] With prompting from the Military Assistance Advisory Group, the Army was once again called upon to provide canine support to allies in the Army of the Republic of Vietnam. The insurgent threat called for an expanded, scout capability and the US Army quickly turned to British advisors who had experience with scout dog employment during the insurgency in Malaysia.[11] Vietnam emphasized canine needs from the USMC, Navy and Air Force as well, who desired dogs not just for scouting, but also security of bases and installations within the theater of operations.[12]

In a 2011 issue of *Infantry Magazine*, author and current US Army MWD Program Manager (PM), Richard Vargus emphasized the loss of continuity in established canine programs of the era, stating: "After the Vietnam War, as after all wars, the MWD program was radically scaled down."[13] A 1990 report from the Army-Air Force Center for Low Intensity Conflict noted similar findings:

> With the end of the Vietnam conflict, general interest in the combat utilization of MWDs faded. The focus of the military's attention returned to heavy combat between major conventional forces on the European continent. The roles of MWDs so laboriously developed and nurtured during the war were ill-suited to the large mechanized and armored combat forces envisioned for the

---

[9] Air Force Office of Scientific Research, 51.
[10] Vargus, 47.
[11] Hammerstrom, 31.
[12] Air Force Office of Scientific Research, 39.
[13] Vargus, 47.

3

future. What interest remained in MWDs was retained by military law enforcement agencies based on their traditional missions.[14]

After Vietnam, the Air Force retained its need for MWD units to defend air bases through the employment of multi-skilled patrol, narcotics and bomb detector dogs, and in September 1983, was designated by the Deputy Secretary of Defense as the DoD Component responsible for the Military Working Dog Program.[15]

THE GLOBAL WAR ON TERROR: DISCUSSION/ANALYSIS

In 2002, the immediate operational need for increased canines in Afghanistan provided the impetus to expand the capabilities of MWDs.[16] Accordingly, as has occurred in every major conflict since WWII, the US Army identified an emerging need for a new war dog skill set to better counter IEDs. While the Air Force was, and continues to be able to provide a C-IED capable MWD to its sister services, the Army desired a capability already being fielded by the United Kingdom and the Israeli Defense Force.[17] Their canines could not only find IEDs, but were also able to locate them at a distance of up to 200 meters ahead of their assigned patrol—an off-leash capability not offered by the Air Force.[18]

When the US-led Coalition of Iraq in 2003 opened up a second theater of operations in USCENTCOM, MWDs were one of a host of C-IED options urgently needed in the field to help minimize losses from the growing threat of IEDs.[19] This need was also recognized by LTG John Abizaid who, when asked during his senate confirmation hearing what his top

---

[14] William Thornton, "The Role of MWDs in Low Intensity Conflict," DTIC Online, Last modified February 2013. http://www.dtic mil/dtic/tr/fulltext/u2/a224049.pdf.

[15] Executive Agent: Department of Defense, Agent: DoD MWD Program, Last modified November 2012, http://dod-executiveagent.osd mil/agentListView.aspx?ID=71.

[16] Pubic Intelligence, "Commander's Guidebook for MWDs", Last modified December 2011, http://info.publicintelligence net/CALL-MWDs.pdf.

[17] JIEDDO, "JIEDDOs Seal: A Tribute to the Past," Last modified January 2013, https://www.jieddo.mil/news_story.aspx?ID=1507.

[18] Richard Vargus, e-mail message to author, 28 April 2013.

[19] JIEDDO, "JIEDDOs Seal: A Tribute to the Past."

priorities as USCENTCOM Commander would be with respect to force protection, responded: "Integrating...military working dogs".[20]

Just over a year after Gen Abizaid assumed command of USCENTCOM in July 2003, the Deputy Secretary of Defense established the "Integrated Process Team (IPT) for Defeating Improvised Explosive Devices (IED)" in an Action Memorandum dated 17 July 2004.[21] In his responding memorandum issued two months later, US Army MG Fred Robinson, Chairman of the IPT, approved the purchase of 39 Specialized Search Dogs (SSD) to deploy to the USCENTCOM AOR in direct support of the IED Defeat Mission. To this end, $6.9M of the FY 2005 Iraqi Freedom Fund was transferred to Air Force Operating and Management budget as the Executive Agent for the Military Working Dog program. Of the nearly $7M allocated to develop an off-leash MWD C-IED capability, the Air Force transferred $1.2M to the Army and $3M to the USMC to fund their satellite test programs varying slightly from the SSD skill-set, while the remainder stayed with the Air Force to fully develop the SSD program at Lackland AFB.[22] (See Appendix A)

On 14 February 2006, DoDDI 2000.19E formalized the C-IED IPT under the DoD, designating it as the Joint IED Defeat Organization (JIEDDO) and defining its mission to, "Focus (lead, advocate, coordinate) all Department of Defense actions in support of the Combatant Commanders' and their respective Joint Task Forces' efforts to defeat Improvised Explosive Devices as weapons of strategic influence."[23] JIEDDO received $3.6B in its first

---

[20] Global Security, LTG Abizaid Senate Confirmation Hearing, Last modified unknown, http://www.globalsecurity.org/military/library/congress/2003_hr/abizaid1.pdf.
[21] Hammerstrom, 119.
[22] Hammerstrom, 119. (Appendix A)
[23] Gordon England, "DoDD 2000.19E," DTIC Online, Last modified February 2006, http://www.dtic mil/whs/directives/corres/pdf/200019p.pdf.

year and currently has approval authority of up to $25M for any single C-IED program.[24] If a program exceeds $25M, but is deemed worthy of funding by JIEDDO, special permission for funding can be quickly obtained from the Deputy Secretary of Defense.[25] In order to ensure the continuity and enduring capability of C-IED war dogs, approval through JIEDDO will likely be the best option now and into the future.

The DoD SSD program, funded by JIEDDO, officially launched in April 2005.[26] (Appendix B) The SSD skill-set is best described by the U.S. Marine Corps:

> Specialized Search Dog (SSD). SSDs are a single purpose MWD that detect IEDs, explosive components, and weapon caches off-leash up to 400m from the handler. SSDs may be utilized to search on leash, but this is **not** [*emphasis added*] the preferred method. SSDs are capable of searching vehicles, buildings, roadways, and open areas. The SSD handler directs the SSD in its search by using hand/arm signals, voice commands directly from the handler or via radio communications, or a combination of the above. SSDs are primarily used in support of the operating force but may be employed in garrison as an explosive detection dog (EDD).[27]

In his April 2006 background paper on SSD production, Mr. Bob Dameworth, DoD MWD PM at the time, highlighted the Army's request to increase its allocation of SSDs to 70 canines per year.[28] (Appendix C) The request originated from an April 2006 memorandum from MG Donald Ryder, Provost Marshal General, who wrote, "SSD teams have proven themselves to be exceptional combat-multipliers in Iraq and Afghanistan and their demand in support of the GWOT is expected to surge."[29] (Appendix D)

The Army request was subsequently fulfilled and a total of 92 SSDs per year were

---

[24] Peter Carey, "JIEDDO: The Manhattan Project that Bombed," Public Integrity, Last modified August 2011, http://www.publicintegrity.org/2011/03/27/3799/jieddo-manhattan-project-bombed.
[25] Carey, NPN.
[26] Doug Miller (DoD MWD Program Manager), e-mail message attachment to the author, 24 April 2013. (Appendix B)
[27] Community Marines, MCO 5580.2B, Last modified August 2008, http://community.marines mil/news/publications/Documents/MCO%205580.2B.pdf.
[28] Doug Miller (DoD MWD Program Manager), e-mail message attachment to the author, 24 April 2013. (Appendix C)
[29] Doug Miller (DoD MWD Program Manager), e-mail message attachment to the author, 25 April 2013. (Appendix D)

allocated for each service from FY07-FY09. (70 for the Army, 4 for the USN, 12 for USMC and 6 for USAF)[30] SSDs and their sister satellite programs, however, could only augment existing on-leash, explosive detection dogs in USCENTCOM. Their production numbers simply were not capable of handling the scope of C-IED missions in the AOR.

IED events climbed steadily to over 4,000 in 2008, but the value of explosive detection dogs was already a proven countermeasure and their continued and increased availability became a CCDR necessity.[31] That same year, the CENTCOM CCDR, Gen David Petraeus, specifically requested an increase in explosive detection dogs in theater, clearly understanding the dependable C-IED capabilities inherent in canines:

> The capability they [military working dogs] bring to the fight cannot be replicated by man or machine. By all measures of performance, their yield outperforms any asset we have in our inventory. Our Army would be remiss if we failed to invest more in this incredibly valuable resource.[32]

Even with the maximum available Army and USMC explosive dogs already deployed in theater, both the Air Force, with the preponderance of explosive detection dogs in the DoD inventory, and the US Navy, regularly filled the void of handlers and dogs assigned outside-the-wire (OTW) missions.[33] It quickly became apparent to the inter-service canine community that the need to exploit the benefits of all explosive dogs in theater outweighed the risks of attaching Air Force and Navy handlers to OTW patrols not previously included in their garrison or pre-deployment mission/training sets, directly challenging the interoperability inherent in the joint force design.

---

[30] Doug Miller (DoD MWD Program Manager), e-mail message attachment to the author, 24 April 2013. (Appendix C)
[31] Craig Whitlock, "Number of U.S. Casualties from Roadside Bombs in Afghanistan Skyrocketed from 2009-2010," *The Washington Post*, January 25, 2011, http://www.washingtonpost.com/wp-dyn/content/article/2011/01/25/AR2011012506691.html.
[32] Public Intelligence, NPN.
[33] Doug Miller (DoD MWD Program Manager), e-mail message to the author, 8 April 2013.

Adding to this challenge were dogs with differing explosive detection capabilities such as differing off-leash effective search ranges, varying numbers of identifiable explosive compounds, etc. The differences between SSDs, its three sister programs and the more common versions of on-leash explosive detection dogs, were not immediately clear to CENTCOM staffers who prepared requests for forces pertaining to canines. The results became evident when the different skills sets arrived in country. Some dismounted patrols worked with SSDs, while others were paired with the standard explosive detection dogs capable of detecting IEDs while on leash only. The varying dogs and mission sets left leadership on both sides of the Atlantic confused about what type of dog to request and employ on missions in USCENTCOM.[34] In retrospect, it seems clear that a baseline capability of an off-leash explosive detection dog provides the best C-IED canine capability for the warfighters assigned to USCENTCOM. Likely due to the limited availability of off-leash capable bomb dogs like the SSD, the USCENTCOM standard requirement remains the same as it's been since its inception; an explosive detection capable canine.

The cycle of ending valuable MWD programs continued when, in July 2009, the Air Force chose to discontinue its service allocation of SSDs, citing excessive training requirements, under utilization, and a preference for dual-purpose explosive detection dogs (on-leash) as they fulfilled both the Air Force garrison and CCDR requirements for explosive detection in USCENTCOM.[35] (Appendix E)

A dual-purpose MWD, as the name implies, is capable of performing multiple tasks. The most common dual purpose MWD used in USCENTCOM is the patrol/explosive

---

[34] Doug Miller (DoD MWD Program Manager), e-mail message to the author, 29 April 2013.
[35] Doug Miller (DoD MWD Program Manager), e-mail message attachment to the author, 24 April 2013. (Appendix E)

detection dog (P/EDD).[36] The 'patrol' portion of the certification means the canine can perform law enforcement functions as well as explosives detection. Air Force Instruction 31-121 best describes the abilities of a patrol certified MWD:

> Law Enforcement. Controlled aggression certified MWDs seek, detect, bite and hold, and guard suspects on command during patrol. They provide a psychological deterrence and can defend their handlers during threatening situations. They can assist in crowd control and confrontation management, and search for suspects and lost personnel, indoors and outdoors.[37]

The Air Force chose to end its service-specific SSD allocations, in part, because SSDs are not dual-certified dogs and, as such, have only limited mission sets when not deployed. The trade-off became the loss of an off-leash capable explosive detection dog that, while no hindrance to the garrison mission, drastically reduced deployed capabilities. Because the off-leash option is not a USCENTCOM requirement, coupled with the fact that off-leash canines are not cost effective or value-added for its garrison mission, the Air Force continues to meet the needs of the CCDR without providing SSDs.[38] The US Navy, allocated the least amount of SSDs among the military branches and the service whose canine mission set most closely mirrors that of the Air Force, never employed their SSDs.[39]

The USMC and USA maintain like-mission sets both in garrison and deployed. They also receive the preponderance of OTW missions and, understandably, prefer the off-leash capable explosive detection canines. Their challenge is two fold: the SSD program was only funded as a wartime requirement and, as such, will end in 2014; the Army and the USMC desire to maintain a like program, but must get it approved and adopted through the DoD

---

[36] 2Lt Gerardo Gonzalez, USAF "When it Comes to Explosives, the Nose Knows Best," *The Tallil Times*, July 11 2003, http://kumite.com/wp-content/uploads/2009/01/20030711-tallil-times-newspaper.pdf.
[37] Doug Miller (DoD MWD Program Manager), e-mail message attachment to the author, 8 March 2013.
[38] Lt Col Joseph Musacchia, USAF (HQ AFSFC/SFOP), e-mail to the author, 23 April 2013.
[39] CW04 Richmond Joslin, USN (Naval Special Warfare, Multipurpose Canine OIC), e-mail to the author, 13 May 2013.

MWD DoD PM, in order to effectively fund and field the program.

Today, every explosives-tasked MWD in USCENTCOM is certified to find IEDs. It is a standard meant to ensure continuity, but instead provides varying degrees of risk. The difference is that some canines in theater can perform the C-IED mission off-leash, providing effective standoff between the device and the dismounted patrol, while others cannot. The results of this incongruity have already been seen in the field.

During a 2012 foot patrol through Helmand Province, Afghanistan, Air Force TSgt Leonard Anderson and his explosive detection dog Azza were embedded with a USA dismounted patrol. Azza was a certified explosive detection dog, but was not off-leash capable. During the patrol, recorded by a professional camera crew documenting MWDs in Afghanistan, a remote-detonated IED exploded, seriously injuring TSgt Anderson.[40] Although it is impossible to determine whether or not an off-leash capable explosive detector dog could have discovered the IED in advance, it is evident that the on-leash MWD cannot provide adequate standoff from a remote-detonated device. This visual evidence most clearly emphasizes the need for a higher standard of C-IED MWDs for the USCENTCOM AOR. It is unfortunate that because of costs, training and misaligned mission sets, elements of the joint community fail recognize the importance of an off-leash capable C-IED canine and choose instead to trade the optimal solution for the acceptable answer.

In her New York Times best selling book, "Soldier Dogs", author Maria Goodavage profiles, among others, the story of USMC GYSGT Kristopher Knight and his MWD Patrick. As an explosives detection dog, Patrick was in high demand in Afghanistan and deployed

---

[40] *Glory Hounds*, directed by John Dorsey and Andrew Stephan (2013; Discovery Channel Communications, Inc, Animal Planet Studios), Amazon Instant Video.

back to back in 2009 and 2010. Goodavage writes, "They deployed to Afghanistan in 2010. Patrick would not make it back alive this time. But everyone else on his final mission would, thanks to this dog and his ability to sniff out bombs without a leash."[41]

Established by the DoD Directive, the Joint Service Military Working Dog Committee (JSMWDC), comprised of the heads of the DoD component MWD programs, review and approve regulations and operational rules for MWD employment across the services. The JSMWDC is required to meet not less than annually to review user requirements.[42] During their November 2012 meeting, the USMC and USA MWD PMs discussed their desires to have the 341 Training Squadron (DoD Military Working Dog School) expand their existing training to develop dual certified, off-leash explosive detection dogs to compensate for the upcoming loss of SSDs.[43] Such a program, if implemented across the services, would effectively provide USCENTCOM a base-line standard for all explosives detection dogs to be off-leash capable. Of particular importance to the Air Force and Navy, the patrol certification would also be present, allowing for practical use in both garrison and deployed missions.

Unfortunately, because the Air Force and Navy do not have written requirements for off-leash explosive detection dogs, coupled with the increased risk to handlers and bystanders that an off-leash, patrol certified MWD would incur (possibly becoming aggressive towards the wrong target), the Air Force as the Executive Agent of the DoD MWD Program, advised the USA and USMC to determine a way ahead for off-leash training

---

[41] Maria Goodavage, *Soldier Dogs* (Dutton: Penguin Group Press, 143).
[42] William J. Lynn III, "DoDD 5200.31E," DTIC Online, Last modified August 2011, http://www.dtic mil/whs/directives/corres/pdf/520031e.pdf.
[43] Doug Miller (DoD MWD Program Manager), *Joint Military Working Dog Committee Meeting Minutes*, 2 November 2012.

11

and submit a coordinated request for a Course Resource Estimate to the 341 TRS. Believing that the Air Force would remain risk averse and that not all patrol explosive detection dogs would be able to achieve off-leash certification, the best option for a joint compromise was tabled.[44] The USA and USMC did, however, engage in a joint field study in an effort to conduct off-leash directional control training for dual certified MWDs at Ft Belvoir as a proof of concept.[45] Their findings were briefed during the April 2013 JSMWDC, when they announced positive tests results for their off-leash dogs at a distance of 100 meters.[46]

Even if the proof of concept continues to yield positive results, it is unlikely that the Air Force will choose to incorporate the training at the 341 TRS because the capability is not required for the Air Force, which owns the vast majority of MWDs and is the DoD MWD Executive Agent (EA). If the 341 TRS does not adopt the off-leash, dual certified MWD training program, no single service has the ability, funding or backing to establish an affordable alternative.[47] And so, once again, a valuable C-IED off-leash capability will likely be lost until the next war when it will be revisited, funded and fielded years after it was first required by the warfighter.

CONCLUSIONS & RECOMMENDATIONS

Clearly, Combatant Commander's understand and appreciate the C-IED abilities offered by MWDs, however, their limited appreciation of potential improvements to existing MWDs precludes the programs ability to best meet the needs of the user. Now is the time to establish a base-line standard of off-leash capable C-IED canines. Providing a less capable

---

[44] Richard Vargus, telephone conversation with the author, 12 April 2013.
[45] Michael Wells (Assistant Program Manager, MWD Program HQ, USMC) e-mail message to the author, 15 March 2013.
[46] Doug Miller (DoD MWD Program Manager), *Joint Service Military Working Dog Committee Meeting Minutes*, 24 April 2013.
[47] Doug Miller (DoD MWD Program Manager), e-mail to the author, 29 April 2013.

canine to the warfighter just because it meets the standard is not in keeping with the highest traditions of the joint force. The USA and USMC cannot field this capability on their own, it must be a joint program and the services must have an appeal authority above the DoD EA for programs they feel best meet the needs of Combatant Commanders. This can be accomplished through improved visibility of MWD experts at the operational level, realignment of the program from an unresponsive OUSD(I), renewed integration with JIEDDO and the timely publication of a DoD manual establishing a capabilities baseline for all DoD explosive detection canines.

Currently, the Chairman, JCS has not designated an OPR to coordinate COCOM MWD requirements as directed in DoDD 5200.31E.[48] Further complicating the lines of communication to the Joint Staff is the location of the DoD MWD PM, who is based at Lackland AFB instead of the Pentagon.[49] This precludes visible, sustained support to the Director, Air Force Security Forces--the Pentagon face of the DoD MWD program. Second and third order effects of this misalignment have likely contributed to extended delays in critical updates to the DoD MWD community. This is best exemplified by the 20-year gap between the publication of the DoD Military Working Dog Program joint instruction published in December 1990 and its successor published in December 2011.

The MWD PMs should be lauded for their desire to publish a manual (*DODM 5200.31, DOD MWD Program*) that will, "establish a capabilities baseline for all types of MWDs produced from the 341 TRS and set the standards for validations in the four

---

[48] LCDR Robert Toth, USN (Joint Staff, J-34/CBRNE) e-mail to the author, 24 April 2013.
[49] Richard Vargus, e-mail to the author, 15 March 2013.

services."[50] Per DoDD 5200.31E, the OUSD(I), is tasked to oversee the DoD EA for the DoD MWD Program by providing for end-user requirements, which makes them the OPR for the manual.[51] Unfortunately, alignment under OUSD(I) has proven to be another structural failure in the MWD organizational hierarchy.

In at least the past two JSMWDC meetings, an OUSD(I) representative has been absent.[52] For an organization to miss an annual meeting for a program they oversee hardly promotes growth and enduring capabilities of their program to Combatant Commanders. Furthermore, as stated in the November 2012 JSMDC meeting minutes, "OUSD(I) Intelligence was not able to make further progress on the DoD Manual."[53] DoDD 5100.01, *Functions of the Department of Defense and its Major Components*, which aligned the DOD MWD PM under OUSD(I) was revalidated in 2010.[54] Sadly, since this was the first revalidation/realignment within the Department of Defense since 1987, it is highly likely OUSD(I) will continue to oversee the DoD MWD EA for the foreseeable future.[55]

If the OUSD(I) is incapable of supporting the DoD MWD EA and the service PMs, it is imperative they relinquish the program to another division within the DoD. The MWD program would make an exceptional fit in OUSD Personnel & Readiness, Law Enforcement program office. Here, the primary beneficiaries of the MWD program would be best positioned to articulate its capabilities, versatility and value to Combatant Commanders.

With Overseas Contingency Operations funds dwindling as the war in Afghanistan

---

[50] Doug Miller (DoD MWD Program Manager), e-mail attachment to the author, 29 April 2013.
[51] Lynn, Enclosure 2.
[52] Doug Miller (DoD MWD Program Manager), e-mail message attachment to the author, 4 March 2013.
[53] Doug Miller (DoD MWD Program Manager), e-mail message attachment to the author, 4 March 2013.
[54] Robert Gates, "DoDD 5100.01," DTIC Online, Last modified December 2010, http://www.dtic mil/whs/directives/corres/pdf/510001p.pdf.
[55] Department of Defense (Odam), Organizational and Management Planning, Last modified unknown, http://odam.defense.gov/omp/Functions/Organizational_Portfolios/Evolution%20of%205100.1 html.

draws to a close, coupled with the added challenges of sequestration, the DoD MWD program must secure funds to prepare for the next war. Hopefully, such funds will be used to expand training at the 341 TRS to include the production of off-leash P/EDDs in support of the C-IED mission—the very baseline the PMs should espouse in their DoD manual.

In order to secure funding, leveraging relationships with JIEDDO is vital. In 2010, after an estimated total of $19B was transferred to it, LTG Michael Oats, the head of JIEDDO, said, "dogs are the best detectors."[56] Today, only three years since that statement, JIEDDO officials now contend, "Among the systems, we still employ the dogs, but we're sort of de-emphasizing them because we find that other technologies are far more effective."[57] MWD experts, the 341 TRS, the media and some members of Congress, however, do not support this opinion.

GYSGT Kristopher Knight, mentioned previously in this paper, currently serves as the Course Chief at the Inter-Service Advanced Skills K9 Course, Yuma Proving Grounds, Arizona. When asked whether he thought MWDs are better than any other C-IED technology being fielded today in Afghanistan, he answered emphatically, "Yes! A well trained Military working dog TEAM is far more efficient than any man-made machine to date; capable of maneuvering over nearly any terrain, doesn't rely on artificial energy, and is able to apply common sense under extreme conditions." He made it a point to emphasize that the key to success is the "TEAM" aspect, adding, "A strong dog is nothing without a

---

[56] Spencer Ackerman, "$19 Billion Later, Pentagon's Best Bomb-Detector Is a Dog," Wired (2010), http://www.wired.com/dangerroom/2010/10/19-billion-later-pentagon-best-bomb-detector-is-a-dog/.
[57] Rowan Scarborough, "Dogs Outdone by Electronic Sensors in Afghanistan," Washington Times, June 6, 2012, http://www.washingtontimes.com/news/2012/jun/6/dogs-outdone-by-electronic-sensors-in-afghanistan/?page=all.

stronger leader."[58]

The 341 TRS projected the production of over 300 trained MWDs for the joint services in FY12.[59] Because of their proven value in the C-IED role, increasing requests for additional MWDs for use in USCENTCOM have prompted the DoD MWD PM to express doubt that the DoD Military Working Dog Training Center will be able to meet their Trained Dog Requirement for FY13.[60]

The media has also challenged the effectiveness of JIEDDOs products, printing headlines like, "$19 Billion Later, Pentagon's Best Bomb Detector is a Dog".[61] In his 2011 article, "People First…and Dogs, Too: A Case Study of Throwing Money and High Technology at a Military Problem," author Dina Rasor blasts much of JIEDDO's costly and now debunked C-IED technology to include the Symphony radio jammer and the Joint IED Neutralizer, espousing:

> Even some of the most conservative members of Congress, such as Rep. Duncan Hunter of the House Armed Services Committee, are angry with the JIEEDO for its mismanagement and low success. He let his anger be known at a hearing on JIEDDO in March, 2010, saying that he believes that many of the programs have failed specifically given how much money was spent. This year [2011], much to the chagrin of JIEEDO and its high-tech camp followers, the agency had to admit that all their billions of dollars devoted to electronic efforts had only worked 50 percent of the time, and that the local insurgency was able to defeat their devices faster than they could come up with new ones. Only one "weapon system" worked 80 percent of the time: dogs.[62]

It is paramount the MWD community prove its C-IED effectiveness to JIEDDO, in part because of a potential funding stream for emerging MWD programs, but also because

[58] Kristopher Knight, e-mail message to the author, 15 May 2013.
[59] Capt Grant Fyall, USAF (AETC 341 TRS DOQ), e-mail message attachment to the author, 11 March 2013.
[60] Doug Miller, e-mail to the author, 10 May 2013.
[61] Ackerman.
[62] Dina Rasor, "People First…and Dogs, Too: A Case Study of Throwing Money and High Technology at a Military Problem," Truth-Out.org, Last modified 26 May 2011, http://truth-out.org/news/item/1287:people-first--and-dogs-too-a-case-study-of-throwing-money-and-high-technology-at-a-military-problem.

JIEDDO reports directly to the Office of the Secretary of Defense Joint Rapid Action Cell, responsible for monitoring, coordinating, and facilitating meeting Combatant Commanders' immediate warfighting needs.[63] Such a platform provides a voice directly from the MWD community to Combatant Commanders. Indeed, JIEDDO may find both renewed legitimacy and longevity for itself through partnering with the 341 TRS and supplementing the increased costs of expanding to P/EDD off-leash certification.

Today, nearly 2,500 MWDs service the DoD.[64] They provide security on military installations around the world, OTW missions in Afghanistan and beside our special operations forces overseas, and they are one of only five Air Force Security Forces (AFSF) Core Capabilities tracked on the Air Force Universal Task List. In 2011, the Director, Air Force Security Forces (AFSF) published the AFSF Master Action Plan 2011-2016. In it, he tasked the MWD component to "revise the DoD MWD Center's handler courses curricula to meet the near and long term needs of the installations and Combatant Commanders".[65]

If this task is to be fulfilled, the MWD EA and PMs must set aside individual service component needs in order to provide for the greater good. They must publish their DoD Manual and promote off-leash, dual purpose P/EDD training within the 341 TRS in order to best provide a base-line standard for Combatant Commanders. They must argue for realignment in the DoD in order to report to those who can best further their initiatives at the Pentagon and they must prove their value to organizations such as JIEDDO in order to ensure longevity in a fiscally constrained environment.

---

[63] JRAC, "Meeting Warfighter Needs for the Asymmetric Threat", DTIC Online, Last modified 25 April 2007, http://www.dtic mil/ndia/2007gun_missile/GMWedGS/ClagettPresentation.pdf.
[64] Doug Miller (DoD MWD Program Manager), e-mail message attachment to author, 12 April 2013.
[65] Air Force Security Forces Center, *AFSF Master Action Plan 2011-2016*, (Brig Gen Jimmy McMillian), NPN, http://afsf.lackland.af mil/Index/AF_A7S-StratPlan2011-2016.pdf.

FINAL THOUGHTS

It is critical to note recent initiatives at the strategic level of war that lend credence for enduring C-IED MWD training. In February 2013, President Obama released a white paper on Countering Improvised Explosives Devices. In it, he called for "finalizing and implementing national guidelines for explosives detection canine teams…coordinating standardized training…and implementing a whole of government approach to integrate agencies at all levels to participate in C-IED activities in order to discover plots to use IEDs in the US or against US persons abroad before those threats become imminent."[66] In light of the recent bombings in the city of Boston and the subsequent activation of Defense Support to Civil Authorities, which was answered by MWDs, the need to provide the most capable C-IED canines becomes even more critically relevant.

---

[66] Barack Obama, "Countering Improvised Explosive Devices," White House, Last modified 26 February 2013, http://www.whitehouse.gov/sites/default/files/docs/cied_1.pdf.

BIBLIOGRAPHY

Ackerman, Spencer. "$19 Billion Later, Pentagon's Best Bomb-Detector is a Dog." Wired. Last modified 2010. http://www.wired.com/dangerroom/2010/10/19-billion-later-pentagon-best-bomb-detector-is-a-dog/.

Air Force Office of Scientific Research. *Conference on Research to Expand the Usefulness of the Military Working Dog, 1970.* Defense Documentation Center, 1971.

Air Force Security Forces Center. *AFSF Master Action Plan 2011-2016.* Last modified 1 March 2011. http://afsf.lackland.af.mil/Index/AF_A7S-StratPlan2011-2016.pdf.

Carey, Peter. "JIEDDO: The Manhattan Project that Bombed." Public Integrity. Last modified August 2011. http://www.publicintegrity.org/2011/03/27/3799/jieddo-manhattan-project-bombed.

Community Marines. "MCO 5580.2B." Last modified August 2008. http://community.marines.mil/news/publications/Documents/MCO%205580.2B.pdf.

Department of Defense. Organization and Management Planning. Last modified unknown. http://odam.defense.gov/omp/Functions/Organizational_Portfolios/Evolution%20of%205100.1.html.

England, Gordon. "DoDD 2000.19E." DTIC Online. Last modified February 2006. http://www.dtic.mil/whs/directives/corres/pdf/200019p.pdf.

Executive Agent, Department of Defense. Agent: DoD Military Working Dog Program. Last modified November 2012. http://dod-executiveagent.osd.mil/agentListView.aspx?ID=71.

Gates, Robert. "DoDD 5100.01." DTIC Online. Last modified December 2010. http://www.dtic.mil/whs/directives/corres/pdf/510001p.pdf.

Global Security. LTG Abizaid Senate Confirmation Hearing. Last modified unknown. http://www.globalsecurity.org/military/library/congress/2003_hr/abizaid1.pdf.

Glory Hounds. Directed by John Dorsey and Andrew Stephan. 2013; Discovery Channel Communications, Inc., Animal Planet Studios. Amazon Instant Video.

Gonzales, Gerardo. "When it comes to Explosives, the Nose Knows Best." *The Tallil Times.* 11 July 2003. http://kumite.com/wp-content/uploads/2009/01/20030711-tallil-times-newspaper.pdf.

Goodavage, Maria. *Soldier Dogs*. Dutton: Penguin Group Press, 2012.

Hammerstrom, Michael. "Ground Dog Day: Lessons Don't Have to be Relearned in the Use of Dogs in Combat." DTIC Online. Last Modified February 2013. http://www.dtic.mil/dtic/tr/fulltext/u2/a442891.pdf.

JIEDDO. "JIEDDOs Seal: A Tribute to the Past." Last modified January 2013. https://www.jieddo.mil/news_story.aspx?ID=1507.

JRAC. "Meeting Warfighter Needs for the Asymmetric Threat." DTIC Online. Last modified 25 April 2007. http://www.dtic.mil/ndia/2007gun_missile/GMWedGS/ClagettPresentation.pdf.

Lynn, William J., III. "DoDD 5200.31E." DTIC Online. Last modified August 2011. http://www.dtic.mil/whs/directives/corres/pdf/520031e.pdf.

Obama, Barack. "Countering Improvised Explosive Devices." White House. Last modified 26 February 2013. http://www.whitehouse.gov/sites/default/files/docs/cied_1.pdf.

Public Intelligence. "Commander's Guidebook for MWDs." Last modified December 2011. http://info.publicintelligence.net/CALL-MWDs.pdf.

Rasor, Dina. "People First…and Dogs, Too: A Case Study of Throwing Money and High Technology at a Military Problem." Truth-out.org. Last modified 26 May 2011. http://truth-out.org/news/item/1287:people-first--and-dogs-too-a-case-study-of-throwing-money-and-high-technology-at-a-military-problem.

Scarborough, Rowan. "Dogs Outdone by Electronic Sensors in Afghanistan." Washington Times. Last modified 6 June 2011. http://www.washingtontimes.com/news/2012/jun/6/dogs-outdone-by-electronic-sensors-in-afghanistan/?page=all.

Shakespeare, William. "Julius Caesar." The Literature Network. Last modified 2012, http://www.online-literature.com/shakespeare/julius_caesar/9/.

Thornton, William. "The Role of MWDs in Low Intensity Conflict." DTIC Online. Last modified February 2013. http://www.dtic.mil/dtic/tr/fulltext/u2/a224049.pdf.

U.S. House of Representatives, *The JIEDDO: DoD's Fight Against IEDs Today and Tomorrow, 2008*. Committee Print, 2008.

Vargus, Richard. "MWDs: A Cost Effective, Low-Tech Answer to a Persistent and Deadly Threat." Infantry, April 2011. http://www.highbeam.com/doc/1G1-278773930.html

Whitlock, Craig. "Number of U.S. Casualties from Roadside Bombs in Afghanistan Skyrocketed from 2009-2010. *The Washington Post*, 25 January 2011. http://www.washingtonpost.com/wp-dyn/content/article/2011/01/25/AR2011012506691.html.

APPENDIX A:
Joint IED Defeat Task Force Memorandum Authorizing Funding for SSD Programs

DEPARTMENT OF THE ARMY
Joint Improvised Explosive Device
Integrated Process Team
400 Army Pentagon
Washington, D.C. 20310-0400

REPLY TO
ATTENTION OF:

28 September 2004

DAMO-OD (IED TF)

MEMORANDUM FOR DEPUTY SECRETARY OF DEFENSE

SUBJECT: Authorization to Release Joint IED Defeat Funds

1. Ref. DepSecDef Action Memorandum "Joint Integrated Process Team (IPT) for Defeating Improvised Explosive Devices (IED)" dated 17 Jul 04.

2. On 27 September 2004, the Joint IED Defeat IPT approved the purchase of 39 Specialized Search Dogs (SSD) to deploy in AOR to support the IED Defeat mission.

3. I approve release of $6,960,000 of FY 2005 IFF funds for the purchase and training of SSD. I asked the USD(C) to prepare the required Congressional notification and funding transfer.

4. Project Manager – The entire amount will be transferred to Air Force O&M, the Executive Agent for the Military Working Dog program. The Air Force will MIPR $1,260,000 to the Army and $3,000,000 to the USMC to fund their satellite test programs. The remainder will stay with the Air Force. The services are responsible for meeting the program parameters set by the IPT on sustainment funding for this project after the bridge funding from the task force is exhausted. Any unused funds will be returned to the Joint IED Task Force.

Fred D. Robinson
Major General, US Army
Chairman, Joint IED Defeat
Integrated Process Team

CF:
SA
VCSA
JIPT Principals

22

APPENDIX B:
Bullet Background Paper on Specialized Search Dog

BULLET BACKGROUND PAPER

ON

SPECIALIZED SEARCH DOG

PURPOSE: Update concerning DoD Dog Center/HQ AFSFC efforts to develop a Specialized Search Dog (SSD) capability for the DoD Military Working Dog (MWD) program

BACKGROUND:
- Immediate need for a specially trained dog team, capable of detecting and marking the presence of Improvised Explosive Devices (IED), arms, ammunition, and explosives at a safe, stand-off distance from its handler
- Current DoD method of employment is on-leash. USA/USMC pursue United Kingdom (UK) (off-leash, 40-50 meter) and Israeli Defense Force (IDF) (off-leash, 150-1000 meters w/radio control capability)
- SSD is an additive to not a replacement of existing EDD capabilities

DISCUSSION:
- USMC Bridge Initiative status:
  - IDF trainers instructed five handler teams—training complete. Initial Operating Capability Feb 05
  - Four Marines attending IDF train the trainer course Feb-Sep 05
  - USMC projects fielding 12 teams in FY 05
- USA Bridge Initiative status:
  - Two SSDs currently deployed
  - Oct 04 started with three students (2 USA/1 USN)--graduated Feb 05
  - Two training classes scheduled for Jan & Jun 05
  - USA projects fielding 15 teams in FY05
- DoD Program status:
  - Course Resource Estimate (CRE) and Resource Requirements Analysis (RRA) finalized Jan 05
  - Phase I training conducted at Lackland AFB, TX, and Phase II at Yuma Proving Grounds, AZ.
  - DoD Dog Center lesson plans finalized and instructors identified Feb 05
  - DoD Dog School purchased candidate dogs Jan 05
  - Funding source required for FY06. HQ/AETC working AMEND POM Special Interest Item for FY07
  - DoD course expects to produce 48 SSD per year
- Funding status:
  - Of total $6,960,000 allocated for SSD, AF received MIPR acceptances from Army and USMC Dec 04 -- $4,260,000 is now obligated
  - Remaining amount will be obligated in the near term

SUMMARY: Program on track—Launch of DOD SSD Program Apr 05

SMSgt Tait/AF/XOS-FP/DSN425-8529/kst/25 Apr 05

23

Appendix C:
Bullet Background Paper on Specialized Search Dog Production Increase

BULLET BACKGROUND PAPER

ON

SPECIAL SEARCH DOG (SSD) PRODUCTION INCREASE

PURPOSE:

To provide update on the current process to increase SSD Team production

DISCUSSION

- The Joint Service Trained Dog Committee (TDRC) meets annually or at the call of the chair. This committee consists of representatives from each service, with decision making empowerment, to speak for their service programs. This group validates or modifies individual service trained dog requirements previously established, starting the second year out from current year and sets requirements for the forth year out. These established requirements are the Air Force's source authority, as Executive Agency, to program for out-year funds needed to purchase candidate dogs.

- In FY05, the TDRC modified/established trained dog requirements as follows

  -- FY07 – 92 (USA-70, USN-4, USMC-12, USAF-6)

  -- FY08 – 92 (USA-70, USN-4, USMC-12, USAF-6)

  -- FY09 – 92 (USA-70, USN-4, USMC-12, USAF-6)

- During the FY04 meeting of the TDRC, the established Army requirement was set at 26; part of the total DoD requirement of 48 through the out-years. The Army requirement was increased to 70 per year in the FY05 meeting of the TDRC. This increase in production will require an increase in Army instructor/trainer cadre from 4 to 13 in order to meet SSD growth identified by Army. This manpower bill has been calculated and validated by the Joint Service ITRO Committee. Provided Army manpower requirements are met, the DoD Dog Center will have no difficulty meeting all DoD trained dog requirements.

- The established increase in SSD production will not generate a requirement for a Course Resource Requirement (CRE) or Resource Requirements Analysis (RRA) as validated by Mr. Bill Willis, HQ AETC/A3L.

Mr. Bob Dameworth/HQ AFSFC/SFOD/DSN 945-5642/rgd/26 Apr 06

24

Appendix D:
Additional Specialized Search Dog (SSD) Training Support/Dog Procurement Request

DEPARTMENT OF THE ARMY
OFFICE OF THE PROVOST MARSHAL GENERAL
2800 ARMY PENTAGON
WASHINGTON DC 20310-2800

REPLY TO
ATTENTION OF

DAPM-MPD-LE

APR 18 2006

MEMORANDUM FOR DIRECTOR OF SECURITY FORCES, HQ USAF/XO, 1340 AIR
FORCE PENTAGON, WASHINGTON, DC 20330-1340

SUBJECT: Additional Specialized Search Dog (SSD) Training Support/Dog
Procurement Request

1. The purpose of this memorandum is to request the Air Force procure additional
military working dogs (MWD) and provide additional training support at Lackland Air
Force Base in order for the Army to increase SSD capabilities.

2. Currently the Air Force provides 24 SSD training slots to the Army annually. This
was sufficient to establish an Initial Operating Capability. However, SSD teams have
proven themselves to be exceptional combat-multipliers in Iraq and Afghanistan and
their demand in support of the GWOT is expected to surge.

   a. In the short term, an additional course in FY 06 for 12 X SSDs is necessary for
the Army to sustain current CENTCOM requirements for OIF and OEF.

   b. The Army also requires 70 MWD and SSD training slots for FY 07 as well as 70
MWD and training slots for FY 08. This increase in MWD procurement and Lackland
training support will allow a transformation of the Army MWD force structure to form a
total of 158 SSDs (121 X Military Police SSDs and 37 X Engineer SSDs) by the end of
FY 08.

3. Your consideration in this matter is appreciated.

4. Point of contact is Mr. Freimarck, DSN 224-6568 or COM (703) 614-6568.

DONALD J. RYDER
Major General, USA
Provost Marshal General

Appendix E:
AF SSD Revisited (Power Point presentation to Director, USAF Security Forces)

Headquarters U.S. Air Force

Integrity - Service - Excellence

AF SSD Revisited

MSgt Robert Tremmel
HQ AFSFC/SFOC

U.S. AIR FORCE

Overview

U.S. AIR FORCE

- Issue
- Current AF SSD Capability
- SSD Program Concerns
- Recommendation

Integrity - Service - Excellence

Issue

U.S. AIR FORCE

- ACC/A7S & 820 SFG/CC recommends eliminating SSD capability from the 820 SFG
- AFSPC does not need/want capability
  - Can conduct mission with current PEDD authorizations
- Contingency Response Groups do not want this capability

Integrity - Service - Excellence

Telecon

U.S. AIR FORCE

- AFSFC: Mr. Ori, MSgt's Tremmel /Cortez, TSgt Lulofs
- AFSPC: Capt Lombardo, MSgt Barrentine
- Malmstrom: Col Probst, Maj Youderian, TSgt Smith
- ACC: MSgt Mack
- CENTAF: MSgt Colombe, TSgt Coyle
- 820th: MSgt Morris
- Minot: Capt Masoner, Chief Watts, SMSgt Jones
- 341 TRS: Mr. Zamarripa, Capt Richeson, Mr. Bunker

Integrity - Service - Excellence

Current AF SSD Position

U.S. AIR FORCE

- Only AF SSD capability maintained at 820th SFG
  - 1 trained SSD handler assigned

  - Unlike traditional MWDs SSD Teams are trained together
  - SSDs are returned to 341 TRS to be trained with a new handler upon handler PCSing
  - Currently there are no SSD slots available to AF for FY10

Integrity - Service - Excellence

SSD Program Issues

U.S. AIR FORCE

- 820 SFG was the Pilot for AF SSDs

- 820 SFG completed zero SSD missions since inception

- CENTAF tried to deploy SSDs
  - 820 SFG claimed they were not ready to deploy

- 820 SFG main concern:
  - SSD Handlers were never programmed

Integrity - Service - Excellence

(Continued on next page)

Appendix E: (Cont.)

SSD Program Concerns
U.S. AIR FORCE

- Loss of patrol capability (P/EDD)
  - P/EDD positions converted to SSD
- SSD training requires handler/dog to return to 341st each time a new team is paired
  - SSD course is 93 days vs traditional handlers course of 55 days
  - SSD can only be handled by SSD handler not traditional handler
- Kennel space to house new SSD authorizations
- Skill set was designed for OTW Jet missions
- Potential for increased JET/RFF deployments

Integrity - Service - Excellence

SSD Employment
U.S. AIR FORCE

- Primary: Support to other services (JET or RFF).

- Possible: conduct PL1/SAMM purges, but this is currently done with P/EDDs

Integrity - Service - Excellence

COA 1
U.S. AIR FORCE

- Maintain/resource SSD Teams for the 820th SFG
  - Pros
    - Tailor SSD training program to meet AF requirements
    - 820th utilize SSDs to clear airfields, new deployment areas, clear potential threat areas (RAF SSDs responsible to clear 5 miles beyond perimeter fence)
    - Mission is best suited to utilize asset properly to its full potential
    - Handlers are on controlled tour, justifying the 6 month training
  - Cons
    - Kennelmaster/trainer will need to spend time working with off-leash teams vice forcing them to train on leash
    - Raising the SSD proficiency level requires training
    - Increase handler numbers to work dogs

Integrity - Service - Excellence

COA 2
U.S. AIR FORCE

- Employ SSD in PL1 Locations
  - Pros
    - SSDs are outstanding assets to clear large areas quickly
    - Single Purpose SSDs acclimate to squad members in area
  - Cons
    - PL1 areas are away from public access; no real SSD benefit
    - Possible SSD JET deployments
    - Length of training course vice time handler will have dog
    - Funds for additional kennel space for SSD

Integrity - Service - Excellence

COA 3
U.S. AIR FORCE

- Remove SSD from Air Force Inventory
  - Pros
    - Eliminate additional Handler requirement for new SSD teams
    - Eliminate additional training req'ts for kennelmaster/trainers
    - Eliminate need for additional kennel space
  - Cons
    - Lose off lead explosive detection capability

Integrity - Service - Excellence

Recommendation
U.S. AIR FORCE

- Remove SSD from the Air Force Inventory
- Move towards expanding current PEDDs capabilities
  - Expand basic Canine Explosive Scent Kit to incorporate additional odors
  - Change training techniques to include long lead detection vs off leash capability
    - Retains patrol capabilities the units want
    - Gives stand-off distance when searching
- PEDDs with expanded capabilities will not require additional schooling and can be worked by any handler

Integrity - Service - Excellence

27

Appendix F:
DoD MWD Organization Chart

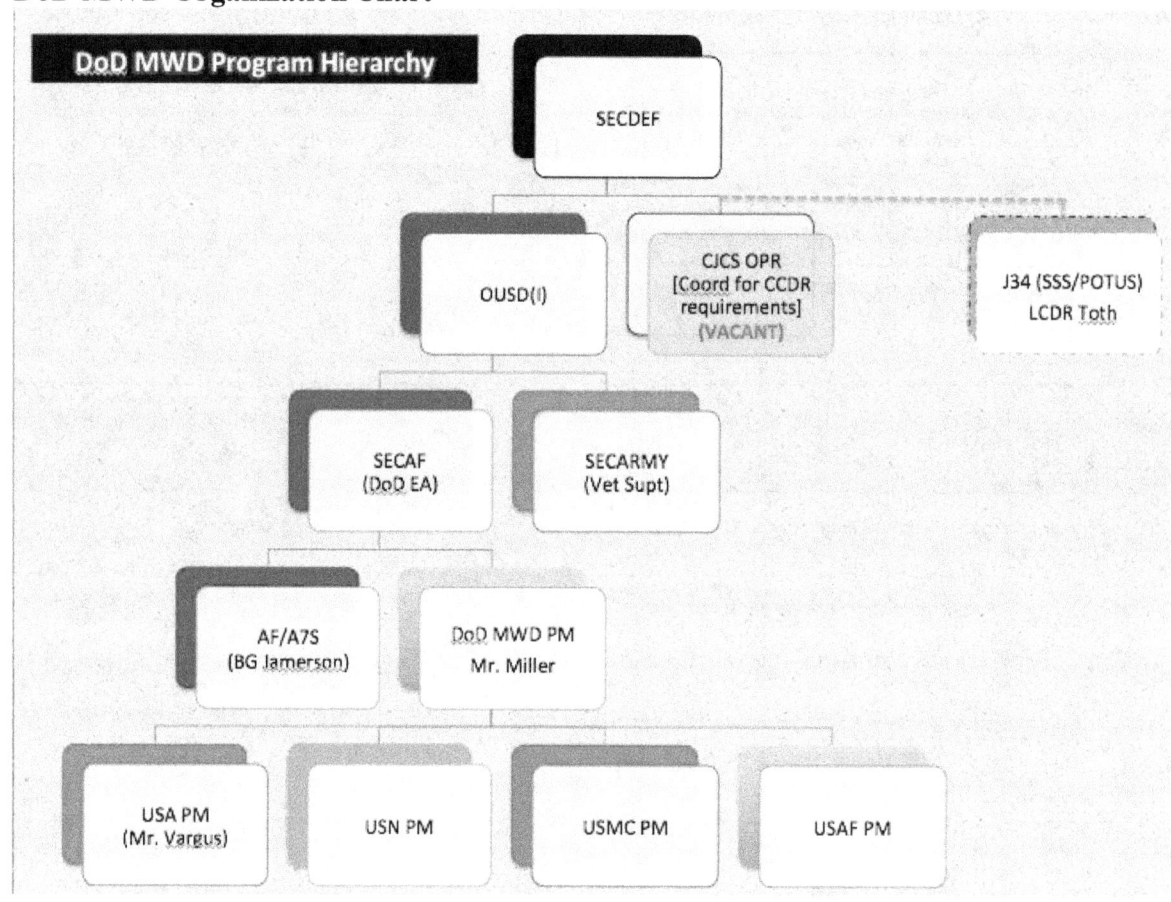

DoD MWD Program Hierarchy

SECDEF

OUSD(I)

CJCS OPR
[Coord for CCDR requirements]
(VACANT)

J34 (SSS/POTUS)
LCDR Toth

SECAF
(DoD EA)

SECARMY
(Vet Supt)

AF/A7S
(BG Jamerson)

DoD MWD PM
Mr. Miller

USA PM
(Mr. Vargus)

USN PM

USMC PM

USAF PM